Last Flight of Angels

poems by

Bruce Majors

Finishing Line Press
Georgetown, Kentucky

Last Flight of Angels

Copyright © 2016 by Bruce Majors
ISBN 978-1-944251-29-1 First Edition
All rights reserved under International and Pan-American Copyright Conventions.
No part of this book may be reproduced in any manner whatsoever without written permission from the publisher, except in the case of brief quotations embodied in critical articles and reviews.

ACKNOWLEDGMENTS

I would like to thank *Number One Magazine, Poetry South, Abyss&Apex, The Medulla Review, Feed Your Brain,* and *Clapboard House* for publishing some of the poems in this book

Grateful appreciation to Cathy Kodra, independent editor in Knoxville, Tennessee, for her encouragement and honest appraisal of my work. Thanks to Stellasue Lee for her work mentorship and advice.

Appreciation to my wife, Patricia, for her help and support in preparing this chapbook.

Editor: Christen Kincaid

Cover Art: "Messengers" by Harold Morrow

Author Photo: Patricia Majors

Cover Design: Elizabeth Maines

Printed in the USA on acid-free paper.
Order online: www.finishinglinepress.com
also available on amazon.com

Author inquiries and mail orders:
Finishing Line Press
P. O. Box 1626
Georgetown, Kentucky 40324
U. S. A.

Table of Contents

Heat Lightning 1

A Certain Chill 2

At the Coffee Shop 3

My Father's Prayer on Sawyer's Hill at the Church of God
    Tabernacle When Revival Came to Town 4

Wild Things 6

Valleys of the Moon 7

What I Know about Light 8

Hall of Mirrors 9

What Saves the Soul from Itself 10

A Cloud of Bees 11

Broken Strand 12

Last Flight of Angels 13

Rainy Day, Imaginary Lover 14

We Are One 15

The Dead Boy 16

Breakfast 17

The Meeting 18

At Night 19

Thanksgiving Day 20

Angels in the Park 22

Patient 24

Night Scene, an Elegy 25

Heavy Breath 26

The Black Unicorn 27

Creation 29

This book is dedicated to the memory of my father and to my grandchildren: Kennedy, Kristian, Taylor, Taylee, Trevor, and Tanner.

Heat Lightning

I lowered the anchor over the side and watched
as the splayed, cast iron behemoth plundered
through green light to the bottom. Waves lapped
boat ribs, making a drowsy, metallic thud.

Pink lightning, forked tongued, struck the western night sky,
threatening ill weather.

Naw, it's just heat lightning, Tom graveled.
Won't bother us.

I thought of electric fences and how lightning coursed
along the wire once, killing a man not ten feet from me.

I thought of my own un-holiness and how
the fires do not purge. I thought of a thousand ways to die.

The heat-cracked night pressed down.
The water, the only certainty. I exist somewhere
between God and my understanding of God.

A Certain Chill

I think it's knowing there is
an end of it all, or the fact
of my uncertainty that meets
me face to face each day.

The future exists only in a series
of backward glances, mostly dim
memories of dreams won and lost.

It is autumn. Early frost, judging
from the caterpillars.
There is a certain chill in the
changing air and in my hollowness.

A young man in a red coat, an old
man in a wool sweater. Recollections
that don't fit into either context.
And still, there's the end of it all.

At the Coffee Shop

They gather each morning around
the table to discuss
nothing in particular, a quartet
        of old men.

There's so much sadness in the world.

With wrinkles and emaciated smiles,
how can they think of anything else?
Their eyes fall on the loneliest
        corners in the room.

Age does not satisfy as we once thought.
With it comes the knowledge
things will not change. We are
not better for having experienced the
        pains of life.

The conversation is sparse on this
cool October morning. As they
sip hot coffee or tea, one or two speak
in low, monotonous voices. Thought
I heard him say cancer, but maybe
        he said censor.

Out on the street, fog had not lifted.
Red lights, barely visible.
Somewhere in the din of invisibility,
a siren screamed, and then another.

Probably been a wreck over on the bypass,
        one old man said.

My Father's Prayer on Sawyer's Hill at the Church of God Tabernacle When Revival Came to Town

The preacher railed and pointed to Heaven,
clouds of holy words spewed from his mouth.
His tongue fluttered and wailed,
many were slain in the Spirit,
others lifted arms and shouted.

Some souls even touched the serpent,
lifted faith to a high fist of venom.
He took us over the edge of fire and back.

Finally, his shirt-soaked sermon finished,
he wiped righteous sweat with white handkerchiefs,
sins washed away.

I was seven years old and
I reckoned that was about as close to hell
as I had been.

And when that anointed saint prayed,
folks fell on hands and knees
before the altar. Mumbled.
Prayers offered up a garbled noise into
moon-silvered night . . .

Dad didn't go. I nudged, he wouldn't go.
He should be there with the others,
praying for us . . . or himself,
I whispered.
God would surely dampen the flames I felt
if Dad would only go . . .

He stared an angry *Stop!* at me,
but the voice in my head spoke in tongues
I didn't understand.

I kept urging—

With malice, Dad went up to face God. He knelt.
Clasped head in hands. Voice like thunder,
he yelled and yelled . . . still the flames burned
around my feet. Dad was doing something
wrong.

That night we were not changed.
Whatever Dad pleaded, God saw fit not to answer.

Wild Things

Out in the fields corn is waist high.
The old tillage tool lies broken with
age. In the grove beyond the pond,
deer lie in the cool shade waiting
for me to leave. Watching my every
movement, measuring my intent.
They don't know I wish them no
harm. Today is my peaceful day.
I could have got them all, oh, all six
lying in the grove, but today is not
for hurting. Today is not for killing
though I could have killed them all.

Something spooked one or two and I watched
as they made high, arching leaps,
retreating to the dark woods at the end
of the corn. Beautiful, those high, graceful
arcs, leaping through pure air in slow motion
floating into nothing but memories.

Turning away, I spot an owl on a tree
limb, rudely staring without blinking. Not as
leery as the deer, he grips his limb
never taking the large, all-seeing eyes from
me, nor I him. Later I saw that same owl
holding a field mouse with one claw and
tearing flesh with his razor beak…*Nothing lasts,*
I thought, *we all must die.*

Valleys of the Moon
> $E=mc^2$
> *Albert Einstein, Visionary*

He needed to see the black disk,
study the golden edges of light slipping out
and what stars might appear.

He needed to know if angels live
there guiding the destiny of brilliant men,
spinning theories for curious men to wonder.

At the place of honored souls,
he needed the illusive prize,
the first to garner the equations,

new thinking, transcendent and bold,
what would anneal science in a modern world,
break the backs of skeptics.

A stoop-shouldered crane
sits on my dock, prehistoric fisherman waiting
for an opportunity in murky water,

losing himself in the gray overcast, merging
elements, not at all unlike God particles
buried within some foggy recess

of Einstein's math. The man could have lost it,
never been completely sure he found it.
Someone would have, though. Crunched

the data and proved the theory. We might have
remained naïve forever, were it not
for those devil angels in the valleys of the moon.

What I Know about Light

Light refracts in a prism, bends
its way through space dispelling darkness,
even darkness gathered around our bodies.
We float there like amber medallions,
flecks of glowing embers.

The milkmaid's path, where she danced,
spilling the light of stars,
is our playground. A handful of brightness,
our medals to bargain with.
Let us tempt angels, we say, *let us fly
through halls of heavenly illumination.*

Neither dark nor light, we tunnel
our way through the ambivalent void
and exist only as something shining
in the universe, like a quarter in a man's pocket.
Small light in a vast darkness.

Hall of Mirrors

> *There is no pain, you are receding*
> *a distant ship, smoke on the horizon*
> Pink Floyd

Walking down the narrow hall, mirrors set
so that it is possible to walk into eternity,
getting smaller and smaller till I do not exist.
The char of burnt-out days, compel me to
this life-maze, uncertain how it ends.

In side mirrors, odd shapes make grotesque
images, how we actually appear without
covers of falseness. Nothing looks the same.
I harbor the thought that none of this is real,
that I am only a dream of some sleeper's
indulgence, a germ of sleep's theater.

I scream *I am alive*.
The long echo resounds through the
mirrors with no answers. No one is there.
I hold my place, footing unsure. A small tapping
at first, rises to a deafening crash, then
the calamity of shattering complexity.

Sleepers awaken, unaware
of night's passing muse. I lie eternally broken
in a thousand shards of glass, my dream
of life unending.

What Saves the Soul from Itself

I walked directly into the blaze of her
anger when I said, *You are too bold.*
She railed against intellectuals who search
for niches where poetry is made
by the bravery of words alone.
You must have meaning,
she barked. *Beauty alone*
means nothing.

I thought about the smooth, round
tumble of words across the tongue,
the fluent collage of innuendos,
the bright images the mind creates.

Meaning, like the meaning of life,
is only explained in beauty, I said.
There are no parallels; only an egress
of events and emotion, years,
and at the end of years, beauty:
survival in a brutal world.
Without it, there is nothing to save.

A Cloud of Bees

Here in this presence of the past,
content to do their work,
a sundown of bees
swarms a fencepost in the orchard.

Soon they'll need a hive.

Dancing the secret latitudes and longitudes
the way to the honey pots
the little circular flights come and go
repeating ancient rituals
keeping nature's sweet promise.

The bees never left what they knew,
never took to the world of loss and regret.

Clover meadow, blackberry, sour wood,
their humming rhapsodies greet the blossoms
of spring, heavy yellow legs dusting
anther and pistil, blessing the fruit of
life in this sacred season.

Walking the fields, wind delivers
the droning thrum to my ears, a song
ferried through the centuries
on the backs of new leaves.

Broken Strand

Out across the lake bed, stumps
appear like bronze castings in
winter's early morning light. Fog
presses down low, curling itself into
the village heart. Far distant crows,
messaging.

Lights in little kitchens come on
late, as if the women there had said:
Wait until this heaviness passes.
Men in stables mend worn leather,
whatever will be needed for spring
plowing.

Farther out on the point, winter water recedes.
Barely outlined, cranes splinter the marsh
as they land.
Blue herons search the edges for minnows,
their stabbing heads like spears slashing
the shallows.

The quietness of fog
vexes me.

Far off the sound of sandhills trumpeting calls
like angels searching for a hidden Heaven.

How will the Christ in them ever find us here,
silent, on this broken strand?

Last Flight of Angels

Sleep drifted away like morning fog.
I dragged myself to the kitchen and drank coffee.

The birds' rattling sounds told me
they were about to leave, heading north.

It's time to go, they seemed to say, *it's time.*

From the back porch, I wrestled goodbyes,
felt saddened beneath their convoluted circling,
as if reciprocating my farewell.

Wave after wave they sailed along the narrow
strand of water, out of sight. The last flight
of angels.

The thundering silence, astounding.

Nothing left but the empty lake bed and,
in the woodlot beyond, the bright,
black murder of crows.

Rainy Day, Imaginary Lover

The tilting rain came fast and hard.
Racing for the barn, too late.
Both soaked in mild October.
You said the rain would cleanse our souls.

The light inside the barn changed itself
in dusty shadows, how it filtered
through sullen clouds to streak the hallway
with luminescence like
the deluge outside.
How sensual the droplets,
silver like dew, that
somehow broke apart
in small blue spatters
and flecked your face.

The quiet patter on the tin roof evoked
an embrace, a kiss, a cloister of passion.
How we locked and separated so easily.
How the magic closed around us.
Imaginary lovers in a day of rain.

We Are One

Docs want to look at my brain,
crack open my head and peer inside.
It makes a sound when I think.

Thoughts pour out as yellow dust,
wooden rattles, bamboo wind chimes
and nightmares.

Together, like cooling lava. Riven,
one side loves music, the other, pain.
We sleep together in each other's dream.

Like Janus faces, a damask rose,
the other, damask steel.

The Dead Boy
for Tommy Roddy

My friend, I thought he said,
his mouth moved slightly, could've said anything.
Ashen, as though he had seen death before.

Tommy got my seat because of a girl
I later married.
In that death chair, riding shotgun,
he was glad I didn't go.

The car did acrobatics off the bridge,
tumbled in the road, broken bodies
catapulted in air, naked bones.

The ditch coiled his body;
he snapped up straight then slumped back.
Crushed. No bones would prop him up.

His eyes dulled, I didn't know what to say
while he died. I think he said, *my friend*.

Breakfast

I was thinking about
this morning
at breakfast when

you said you didn't
really care anymore,
how fragile the

plates were and
how delicate the
tiny flowers

around the borders,
when you said
you thought we

needed to be apart, how
the tablecloth had
a spot and how it

didn't seem to fit,
how the room slid
to one side.

The Meeting

They meet each day in the hall.
Nothing more.
She has a quiet beauty,
a presence. Dark eyes.

Secretly he loves her though
he cannot say it. They
live in different worlds.

Today his expression,
as they pause to say hello, pinched,
pale, almost choked.

*What, she said? Is something
wrong?*

Yes, he said. *Everything*.

At Night

I hate getting up at night
peering into darkness,
seeing yellow remnants
of dreams,
wondering what's there,
feeling my way along walls
room to room,
familiar objects passing like
old acquaintances,
trembling myself toward
some small light I only imagine
to be light
dim to my adjusting eyes,
shuffling myself along,
careening into the abyss
of an old chair
stuffed with memories.

Thanksgiving Day:
> *A Surreal Look at Death*
> *(For two voices)*

(1)

Tonight the dark man slips in
like a thief
over me.
                                        I cannot see.

Tonight I heard the scratching
of the whisper man,
his black muzzle pressed against my window.
                                        The dark wish stands before me.
                                        Weeping winds heave into.

(2)

Darkness slides over me,
into me. Toward night.

                                        Dark faces looking back,
                                        fading to a slap
                                        of white caps
                                                    spreading into the hillside.

A wonder of wind
blown into summer.

                                          The night of weeping wind.

I can be more specific:
It is to roll the blanket of stars,
climb into halls of empty air
that I have come to this point.

                         It is to rake at the wall of darkness
                         gathering behind my eyes,
                         the hollow of air
                         listens me into.

(3)

A stronghold of snakes.
There, the floor moves,
rears up into night.

                         Galaxies, a thousand galaxies.

(4)

Out by the gate bluebells are in full season,
hummingbirds hover
at thirty thousand beats per minute.

                         The bloody rose punishes the trellis.

Underneath, half covered with petals,
a tiny wing bone.

(5)

The dark man enters the gate.   The dark man enters the gate.
                                           He enters the night gate,
                                           listens me into . . .

Angels in the Park

The leaves are somber,
rattling through emptying branches,
spinning a dance improvisation
between the November sky
and mottled earth. The park is
empty except for lovers, here and there,
looking lost and
alone.

Leaves gush like rushing rivers
in the wind across dry ground,
 and the only sound is their sound
 and the sound of wind
 they make together, a weeping sound
like all the tears winter can gather
and pour into a dreary afternoon.

The angels inherit the leaves
and the wind
and the freezing lovers.
The little stone angels
that lie broken here and there,
half covered, wings chipped,
the same immutable almost-
smiles to last for eternity.

I thought I saw a rose
in her hand. Were they rose petals
falling or blood pouring down the
stems of arms?
And the hands the lovers held
were briars. They bled and hurt.
Faces scratched when they touched,
and their pain filled the afternoon.

The angels watched dispassionately,
no feel for love or pain,
no sharp drop from Heaven.

Patient
For my Dad

The first thing is the smell;
medicinal, mercuric,
a kind of sterile disinfectant
which dissolves even
the most hopeful thought.

I.V. meters click away hours,
sharp needles reconcile pain,
grim faces in hospital garb
tell it like it is.

Suffering preambles death.
Pain is bipartisan.
Family whispers in hallway,
leaving a small dejected man
to worry alone.

Night Scene: An Elegy
For Bruce Majors Sr.

Night, black wolf stalking red eyes
of the horizon, must be little cities there.

He roams, pressing wet muzzle
against window panes where patients hide
and against window panes of the tall
building where pain hides.

Blinking lights surround beds
with lab coats twirling needles,
death so close no one dares to breathe.

Old women turn their heads and cry.

Repeatedly the sandman comes with noxious sleep.
In white jacket and surgical mask,
he bears vague predictions.

Is it not enough? I cried.
Dear God, is it not enough?

Heavy Breath

For weeks I have been unable to function as an adult,
shadows of winter hiding behind the barn.

I walked the knobs to Swafford pond in the lower hollow.
There was nothing there for me.

Small lights blink along Walden Ridge to the west
as the sun draws its last heavy breath. I am left

alone with night bugs, barn owl, and the heavy oak
whose acorns have already begun to drop.

The Black Unicorn

The clock hanging on my drawing room wall
never sounded so loud
the eccentric ticking monotonously reminds me
of days past. I tell myself the terrible days are passed.

Ghosts share this silent house, their tiny sounds
personified by the noise of age and failing wood.
Floorboards moan with each step. I scrape
my feet along, mostly to hush the boards,

Listen, Spirit noise: a small ringing in the ears or shredded voices in
the hum of telephone wire, cloudy and distant.
    The illusive blessing was never conferred, they chant.
    Love was an obstacle that couldn't overcome, they whisper.
Ghosts still haunt those gilded relations.

My other self chimes in at the sound of the clock.
And we digress to endless possibilities.
I talk to myself, a sign of dementia,
but it's these damned voices that keeps me remembering.

When I was a boy I had a magic horse,
a unicorn, black as the darkest thought.
Made of rags, he carried me away from quarrelling,
rants, flying fists and angry eyes,
to secret gardens where I could be safe from turmoil.
Later, older, we went to smoky places with Indian lutes,

and theaters where recklessness was the main attraction.
I flew away from melancholy, built walls. Painful walls.
This house has become a dreary refuge, an old horse,
skin glistening with sweat, and hip bones showing.

The shrinks reckoned: *dysfunctional home, make believe,
dark swimming dreams.* When they asked me about the horse,
I told them everything, where every dream and nightmare
was buried. . . I still hear the voices.

Creation

Silken weave,
spun with morning dew,
burns cool in first sun,
hung like diamonds
around the stem of royalty.

Tiny spider,
do you know
what treasure you possess?

Nothing less
than the artistry of God.

Bruce Majors, a native of Tennessean, has published poems in *Pirene's Fountain, Ontologica, Wordgathering, Arts and Letters, Pinesong, The Distillery, River Poets Journal, Number One*, and other literary journals. His collection, *The Fields of Owl Roost*, was named finalist in the 2005 Indie Excellence Book Awards. A chapbook, *Small Patches of Light*, was published in September 2013 by Finishing Line Press. A second chapbook is scheduled for publication in October 2015. Majors co-edited the anthology, *Southern Light, Twelve Contemporary Southern Poets* which included such poets as Robert Morgan, Dan Powers, and Bill Brown. Mr. Majors is a member of the Chattanooga and Knoxville Writers' Guild.

www.ingramcontent.com/pod-product-compliance
Lightning Source LLC
Chambersburg PA
CBHW051705040426
42446CB00009B/1312